## Acknowledgments

I am grateful for Tim Roof's experienced advice. This project wouldn't have been possible without the continued love and support from Eliane Samson. My friend Richard Weiss provided both encouragement and thoughtful suggestions. I am indebted beyond easy measure to the teachers, as well as the readers and students with whom I have shared life or work and joy, and from whom I learned much.

Is this a William Morris Design?
No, these wriggling worms are crystallized Vitamin C under a microscope.

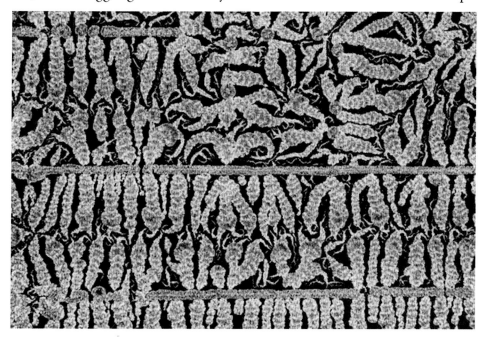

Copyright © 2014 by Jason Christopher Lehman

Leonardo da Vinci claimed that if he watched clouds long enough he could see all of life in the passing of clouds overhead.

Einstein believed that while we all view the same things, we all perceive those same things differently.

A sixteenth century painter Giuseppe Arcimboldo composed human portraits assembled from vegetables, fruits, and flowers. Legend has it that while he was washing his fruits and vegetables he saw a vision of art. Was he an accidental artist? That is what this book is about. It's a new way of looking and seeing. It's fun to look at the world with a new eye; hunting for art with everyday objects. Looking and seeing can be two entirely different things. While clouds may literally change their shape in the sky, it is also possible for us to create "change" in our minds eye—just by the way we choose to look at the wondrous natural objects around us.

In a sense, everything we look at is a kind of Rorschach pattern: we see what our unconscious mind wants to see. The ginseng root has captured the imagination of many cultures for thousands of years, undoubtedly owing to its uncanny resemblance to the human body. Is the ginseng root a natural piece of art? I think so.

Anyone can practice and learn this new way of seeing from the old to the young and from all the countries of the world with any educational level. In our environment we are surrounded with man made objects that often have striking resemblances to living things. Most classic theories of art prescribed holding a mirror up to nature for the artists truest inspirations. The following collection is presented as examples where nature has become the artist itself. The author invites you to enjoy this group of photographs and encourages you to tune in to the Accidental Art around us everyday.

Outer-space reflected on Main Street.
A supernova explosion creates a nebula.
Here an oil leak creates a nebula.

Jackson Pollock, what do you think?
Black crows created this masterpiece.

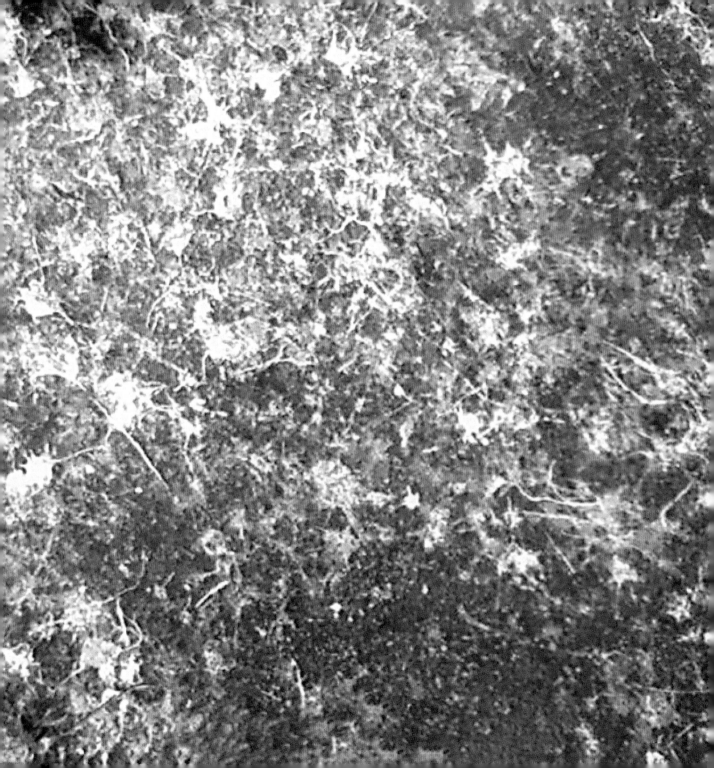

A Painters Maze.
A man walked through this maze
while painting his home.

The lips of Hades kissing our world through
the floor of a pizza shop in Rome.

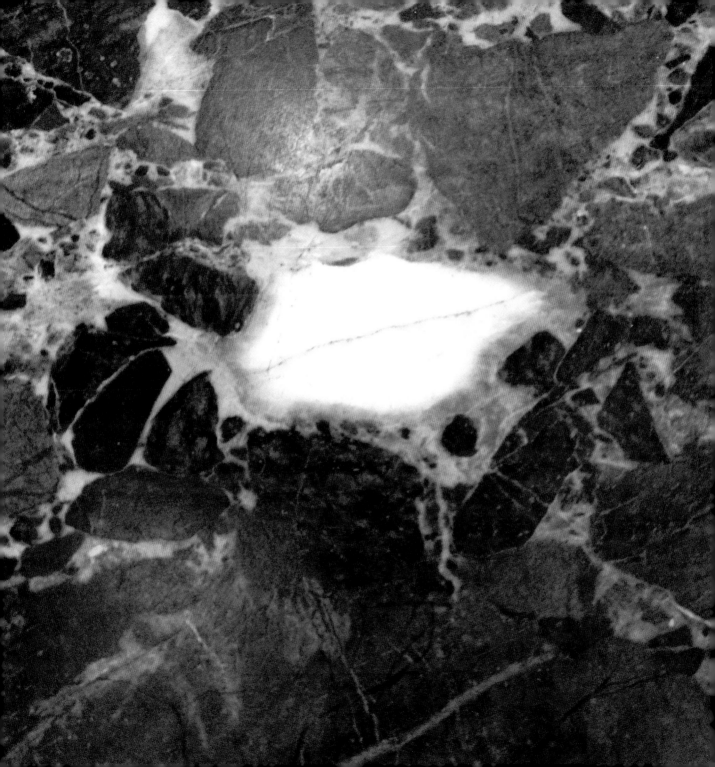

Different rates of evaporation have created this master work on the wall of an Episcopalian church. What will the wall look like after 40 days and 40 nights of rain? Do you see the stiletto shoe?

Which came first the rock or *The Thing?* Could this rock have been the inspiration for Stan Lee's fictional character, *The Thing,* of Marvel Comics fame?

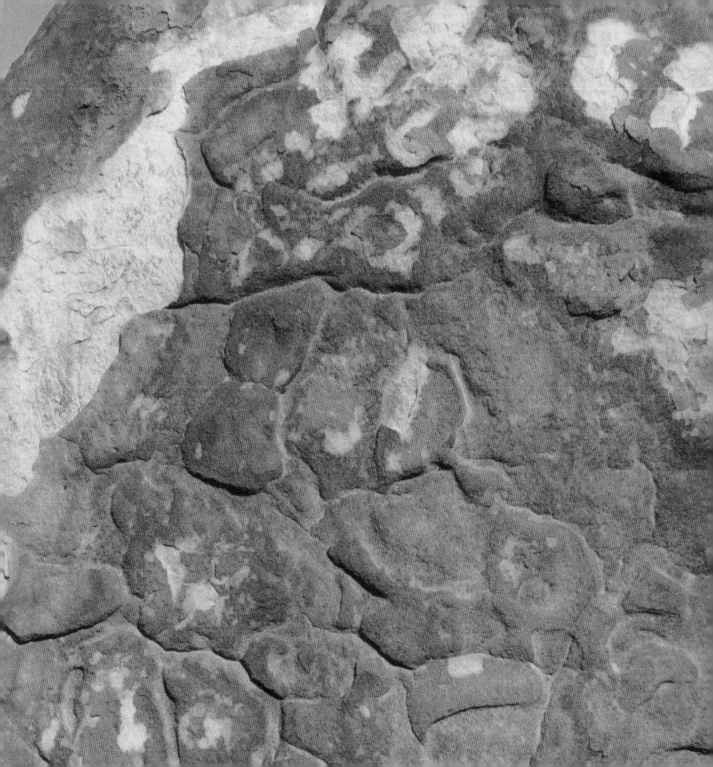

Galaxy girl! Freckles can be found on anyone. A freckle is also called an ephelis. This lovely girl has freckles over ninety percent of her body. Many of her freckle patterns match constellations. Galaxy girl!

Rusty squares! Random rusty squares! A rusty filing cabinet moved periodically created this geometric masterpiece. Notice the extraterrestrial faces joined at the nose possibly readying for a kiss.

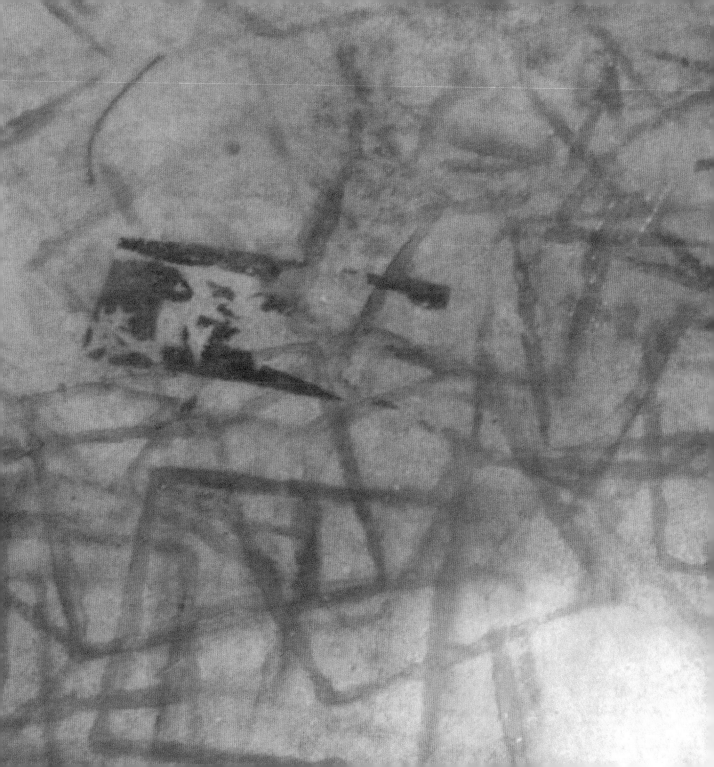

Tar sealed street cracks. String theory involves quarks, hadrons, protons, and neutrons. The quark got its name from a famous quote in James Joyce's novel, *Finnegans Wake.*

A weathered tunnel in Los Angeles. Do you see a fish
on a line in the center? Some people see an ear.
I see an alien to the left.
And you? What do you see?

A paint spill on pavement is similar to a streaking comet moving through space at 56,000 miles per hour.

The mountain's massive heart is reaching up to the Heavens.
It might be tough to break this heart.

The speed of light is 186,282 miles per second.
Light travels around the Earth 7 times per second.
This rubber light pole base protector is similar to light traveling.

A leaking milk or paint truck paints the image of a Comet's tail. It's a Milky Way, created by what looks to be milk splashed then frozen upon a willing asphalt canvas.

Light through my thumb and forefinger. Or, a possible opening to another dimension. Light is electromagnetic radiation that is visible to the human eye, and it is responsible for the sense of sight.

In certain cultures when an arrow is pointed to the left it meant warding off evil, pointing to the right meant protection and an arrow pointing down meant peace. The arrow on the opposite page is pointing up. What does an up pointing arrow mean to you?

Jellyfish on pavement. Jellyfish are found in every ocean. They are the oldest multi-organ animal on Earth. Galaxy IC-3418 is in the shape of a jellyfish.

This image suggests a Solar System nestled in an infinity of sand, just as our Solar System floats in an endless sea of stars.

This may be the first trace of alien blood on Earth.

The Great Sphinx of Giza, Egypt is the largest monolithic statue in the world. It sits on the west bank of the Nile River. Here is the Sphinx of Las Vegas at Red Rock Canyon National Conservation Area in Las Vegas.

Yellow brain being crushed.

This masterpiece was uncovered as a gentlemen removed
branches from a wall preparing it  for painting.
Reveal: Headless stick figure with tail walking.

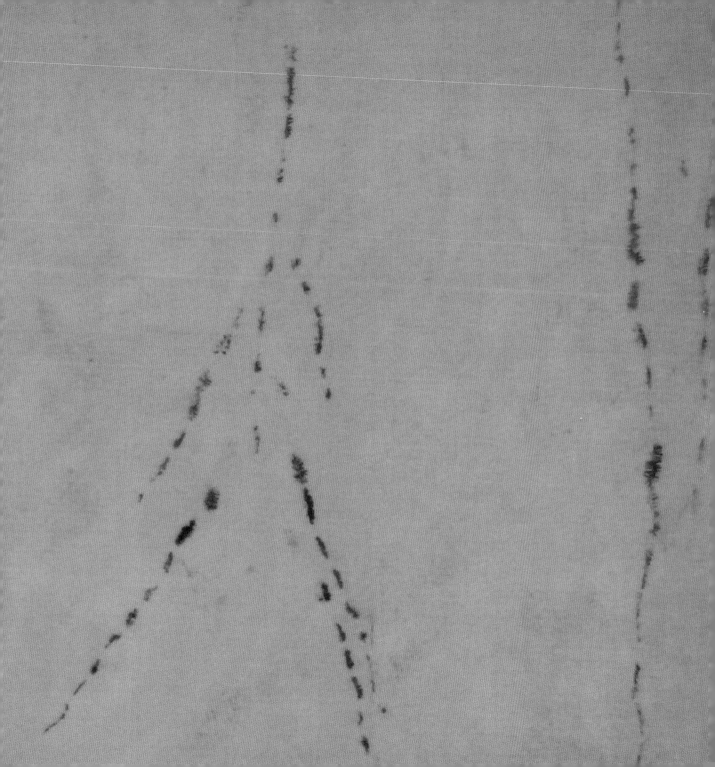

This wall boasts a patina of pennies.
A copper tapestry transforms a blank wall into a tribute to Abe Lincoln.
How many cents are on the opposite page? Are you counting?

Red figure eight.

Now it's your turn. Take a chance. Label this piece of Accidental Art.

Back cover image:
Interstellar Space
Pavement that has been etched by the undercarriages of vehicles
is similar to interstellar space.

Email your images of Accidental Art to: jasonlhmn@yahoo.com

Mail your images of Accidental Art to:
Jason Lehman
PO Box 91703
Santa Barbara, Ca 93190

Library of Congress Number: 2014909229